FM 30-39

BASIC FIELD MANUAL

MILITARY INTELLIGENCE

IDENTIFICATION OF
ITALIAN AIRCRAFT

Prepared under direction of the
Chief of Staff

UNITED STATES
GOVERNMENT PRINTING OFFICE
WASHINGTON : 1941

WAR DEPARTMENT,
WASHINGTON, October 24, 1941.

FM 30-39, Military Intelligence, Identification of Italian Aircraft, is published for the information and guidance of all concerned.

[A. G. 062.11 (8-9-41).]

BY ORDER OF THE SECRETARY OF WAR:

G. C. MARSHALL,
Chief of Staff.

OFFICIAL:

E. S. ADAMS,
Major General,
The Adjutant General.

BASIC FIELD MANUAL

MILITARY INTELLIGENCE

IDENTIFICATION OF ITALIAN AIRCRAFT

The material contained in this manual has been secured from many sources. It is the best material available but may be incomplete and, in some respects, inaccurate.

This manual containing illustrations with explanatory data relative to Italian aircraft is published for limited distribution. It will be used for instruction of officers and men in appearance and general characteristics of Italian aircraft.

The Italian airplane markings are as shown below:

Wing

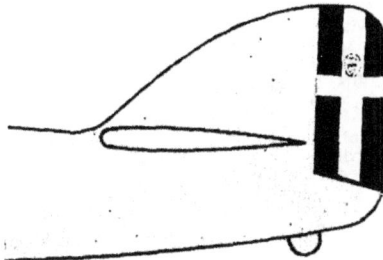

Tail

ILLUSTRATIONS

LAND PLANES:
  Fighters: Page
    A. U. T. 18 (Umbra)_____ 4
    Breda 64_____ 6
    Caproni CA 165_____ 8
    Caproni Vizzola S. A. F. 5_____ 10
    Fiat CR 32_____ 12
    Fiat CR 41_____ 14
    Fiat CR 42_____ 16
    Fiat G 50_____ 18
    Macchi C 200_____ 20
    Meridionali RO 41_____ 22
    Meridionali RO 51_____ 24
    Reggiane RE 2000 "Falcho I"_____ 26
  Fighter-bombers:
    Breda 65_____ 28
    Savoia Marchetti SM 85 (dive)_____ 30
  Bombers:
    Breda 88_____ 32
    Caproni CA 311 (reconnaissance)_____ 34
    Cant Z 1007 bis_____ 36
    Cant Z 1011_____ 38
    Caproni CA 135 bis_____ 40
    Fiat BR 20_____ 42
    Fiat CR 25_____ 44
    Piaggio P 32 MK II_____ 46
    Savoia Marchetti SM 79 (reconnaissance_____ 48
    Savoia Marchetti SM 81 (reconnaissance)_____ 50
  Reconnaissance:
    Caproni CA 111_____ 52
    Caproni CA 310 Libeccio (bomber)_____ 54
  Army cooperation:
    Caproni CA 134_____ 56
    Caproni CA 164_____ 58
    Meridionali RO 37 bis_____ 60
  Transports:
    Caproni CA 133_____ 62
    Fiat G 18_____ 64
    Savoia Marchetti SM 73_____ 66
    Savoia Marchetti SM 75_____ 68
    Savoia Marchetti SM 82 "Marsupiale"_____ 70
    Savoia Marchetti SM 79 (reconnaissance)_____ 48
  General purpose:
    Caproni Ghibli_____ 74
    Nardi F. N. 315_____ 76
SEAPLANES:
  Fighters:
    Meridionali O 44_____ 80
    Meridionali RO 43 (reconnaissance)_____ 82
  Reconnaissance-bombers:
    Cant Z 501_____ 84
    Cant Z 506B_____ 86
    Caproni CA 312 bis_____ 88
    Fiat R. S. 14_____ 90

IDENTIFICATION OF ITALIAN AIRCRAFT

LAND PLANES

ROYAL ITALIAN
AIR FORCE

A. U. T. 18 (UMBRA)

Description:	Round tip, tapered, slightly dihedral, low-wing monoplane. All metal, single motor, enclosed cockpit, blunt nose, retractable landing gear.
Crew:	1.
Armament:	2 medium caliber machine guns in fuselage.
Ammunition:	
Bomb load:	
Radio:	
Armor:	
Motors:	1 Fiat A 80 RC. 41, 1,000 horsepower.
Maximum speed:	304 miles per hour.
Rate of climb:	
Service ceiling:	
Maximum range:	
Wing span:	38 feet.

Fighter
A. U. T. 18 (UMBRA)

ROYAL ITALIAN
AIR FORCE

BREDA 64 FIGHTER

Description: Round tip, tapered, slightly dihedral, low-wing
monoplane. All metal, single motor, en-
closed cockpit, blunt nose, retractable
landing gear.

Crew: 2.
Armament:
Ammunition:
Bomb load:
Radio:
Armor:
Motors:
Maximum
  speed:
Rate of
  climb:
Service
  ceiling:
Maximum
  range:
Wing span:

6

Fighter
BREDA 64

ROYAL ITALIAN
AIR FORCE

CAPRONI CA 165

Description:
Crew:
Armament:
Ammunition:
Bomb load:
Radio:
Armor:
Motors: One 900 horsepower.
Maximum
   speed: 280 miles per hour.
Rate of
   climb: 23,000 in 8.2 minutes.
Service
   ceiling: 32,800 feet.
Maximum
   range:
Wing span:

Fighter
CAPRONI CA 165

ROYAL ITALIAN
AIR FORCE

CAPRONI VIZZOLA S. A. F. 5

Description:	Low-wing monoplane. All metal fuselage, wood wings, enclosed cockpit, single motor, fairly long blunt nose, retractable landing gear.
Crew:	1.
Armament:	2 medium caliber machine guns in sides of fuselage firing through propeller.
Ammunition:	
Bomb load:	
Radio:	
Armor:	
Motors:	1 Fiat A. 74 RC. 38, 840 horsepower.
Maximum speed:	
Rate of climb:	19,680 feet in 6.3 minutes.
Service ceiling:	31,160 feet.
Range:	373–620 miles.
Wing span:	37 feet.

IDENTIFICATION OF ITALIAN AIRCRAFT

Fighter
CAPRONI VIZZOLA S. A. F. 5

ROYAL ITALIAN
AIR FORCE

FIAT CR 32

Description: Round tip, staggered, straight-wing biplane of
              unequal span. Pointed nose with cooling
              radiator beneath single motor. Fixed land-
              ing gear, open cockpit, fabric covered.
Crew: 1.
Armament: 2 Vickers machine guns in top cowling firing
              through propeller.
Ammunition:
Bomb load:
Radio:
Armor:
Motors: 1 Fiat A. 30 R.A., 550 horsepower.
Maximum
  speed: 242 miles per hour.
Rate of
  climb: 19,680 feet in 11 minutes.
Service
  ceiling: 26,240 feet.
Range: 525 miles.
Wing span: 29 feet.

Fighter
FIAT CR 32

ROYAL ITALIAN
AIR FORCE

FIAT CR 41

Description: Round tip, staggered-wing biplane of unequal
span. Upper wing slightly gull wing. Single
motor, blunt nose, open cockpit, fixed landing
gear.

Crew: 1.
Armament:
Ammunition:
Bomb load:
Radio:
Armor:
Motors: 1.
Maximum
  speed:
Rate of
  climb:
Service
  ceiling:
Range:
Wing span:

Fighter
FIAT CR 41

ROYAL ITALIAN
AIR FORCE

FIAT CR 42

Description:	Round tip, straight-wing biplane of unequal span. Fuselage metaled forward, fabric aft. Fabric wings, single motor. Fairly long blunt nose, open cockpit, fixed landing gear.
Crew:	1.
Armament:	2 machine guns in fuselage firing through propeller.
Ammunition:	
Bomb load:	
Radio:	
Armor:	
Motors:	1 Fiat A. 74 R1C 38, 840 horsepower.
Maximum speed:	279 miles per hour.
Rate of climb:	19,680 feet in 7 minutes.
Service ceiling:	31,300 feet.
Range:	
Wing span:	31.9 feet.

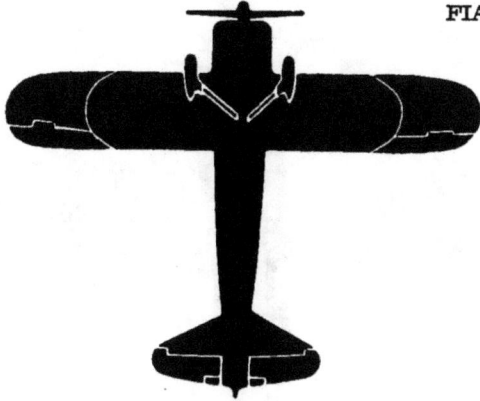

ROYAL ITALIAN
AIR FORCE

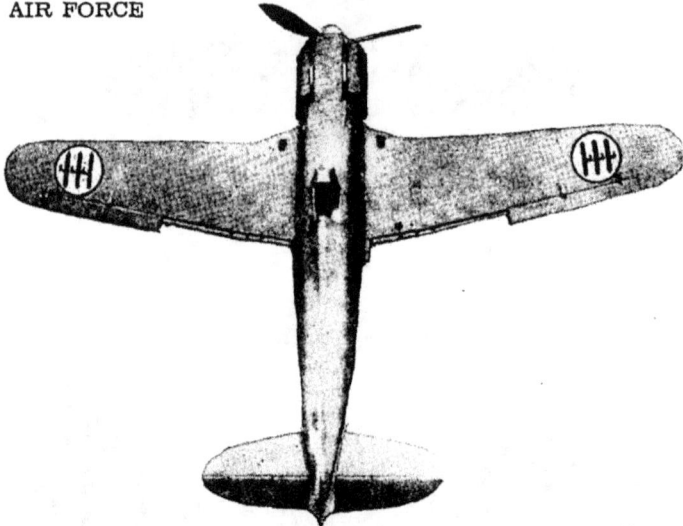

FIAT G 50

Description:	Round tip, very slight forward sweep, slightly dihedral, long-wing monoplane. All metal, single motor, enclosed cockpit, blunt nose, retractable landing gear.
Crew:	1.
Armament:	2 fixed machine guns in top of fuselage firing through propeller; 2 fixed in wings firing outside of propeller.
Ammunition:	
Bomb load:	36 3-kg or 144 1-kg bombs.
Radio:	
Armor:	
Motors:	1 Fiat A. 74 RC. 38, 840 horsepower.
Maximum speed:	299 miles per hour.
Rate of climb:	16,400 feet in 5.2 minutes.
Service ceiling:	35,430 feet.
Range:	435 miles.
Wing span:	35½ feet.

18

Fighter
FIAT G 50

ROYAL ITALIAN
AIR FORCE

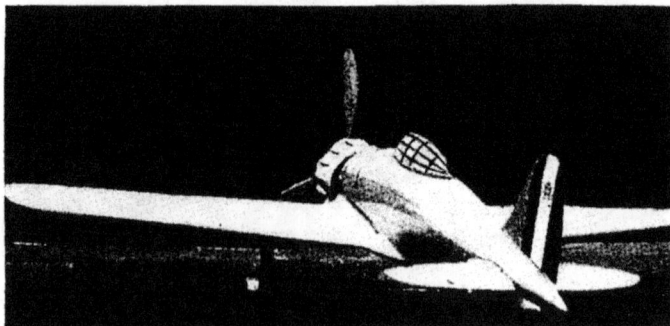

MACCHI C 200

Description: Round tip, slightly swept-back, slightly di-
               hedral, low-wing monoplane. All metal, sin-
               gle motor, enclosed cockpit, blunt nose,
               retractable landing gear.
Crew: 1.
Armament: 2 fixed machine guns in cowling firing through
               propeller.
Ammunition:
Bomb load:
Radio:
Armor:
Motors: 1 Fiat A. 74 RC. 38, 840 horsepower.
Maximum
   speed: 313 miles per hour.
Rate of
   climb: 19,680 feet in 6.5 minutes.
Service
   ceiling: 32,470 feet.
Range: 435 miles.
Wing span: 34⅔ feet.

Fighter
MACCHI C 200

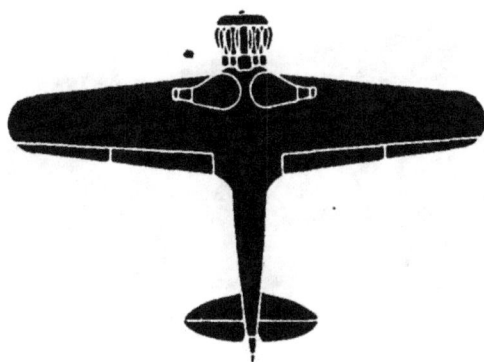

21

ROYAL ITALIAN
AIR FORCE

MERIDIONALI RO 41

Description:	Round tip biplane of unequal span. Upper wing slightly gull wing. Single motor. Blunt nose, open cockpit, fixed landing gear.
Crew:	1.
Armament:	2 Breda-Safat machine guns firing through propeller.
Ammunition:	
Bomb load:	
Radio:	
Armor:	
Motors:	1 Piaggio P. VII C. 45, 390 horsepower.
Maximum speed:	211 miles per hour.
Rate of climb:	19,800 feet in 8.5 minutes.
Service ceiling:	24,500 feet.
Range:	
Wing span:	29 feet.

22

Fighter
MERIDIONALI RO 41

ROYAL ITALIAN
AIR FORCE

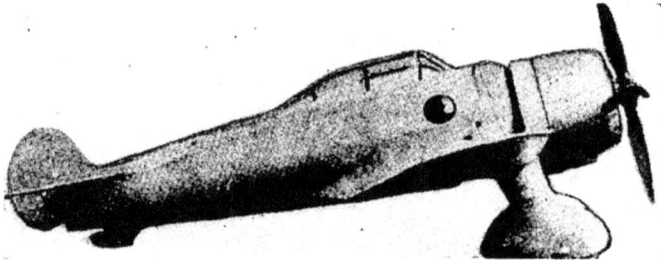

MERIDIONALI RO 51

Description: Round tip, tapered, slightly dihedral, low-wing
monoplane. Metal clad fuselage, single mo-
tor, fairly long blunt nose, enclosed cockpit,
retractable landing gear.
Crew: 1.
Armament: 2 Breda-Safat heavy machine guns firing
through propeller.
Ammunition:
Bomb load:
Radio:
Armor:
Motors: 1 Fiat A. 74 RC. 38, 840 horsepower.
Maximum
speed: . 317 miles per hour.
Rate of
climb: 19,680 feet in 7 minutes.
Service
ceiling:
Range:
Wing span: 32¼ feet.

Fighter
MERIDIONALI RO 51

ROYAL ITALIAN
AIR FORCE

REGGIANE RE 2000 "FALCHO I"

Description: Round tip, tapered, slightly dihedral, low-wing
monoplane. All metal, single motor, blunt
nose, enclosed cockpit, retractable landing
gear.

Crew: 1.

Armament: 2 heavy machine guns mounted on the wings
clear of the propeller.

Ammunition:

Bomb load:

Radio:

Armor:

Motors: 1 Fiat A. 80 RC. 41, 1,000 horsepower.

Maximum
speed: 350 miles per hour (approximate).

Rate of
climb: 19,680 feet in 6.3 minutes.

Service
ceiling: 36,900 feet.

Range: 3 hours.

Wing span: 36¼ feet.

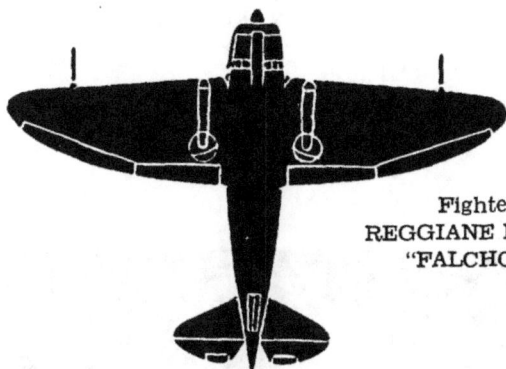

Fighter
REGGIANE RE 2000
"FALCHO I"

27

ROYAL ITALIAN
AIR FORCE

BREDA 65

Description:	Round tip, tapered, slightly dihedral, low-wing monoplane. All metal, single motor, enclosed cockpit, blunt nose, retractable landing gear.
Crew:	1 or 2.
Armament:	5 machine guns; 2 12-mm and 2 7.7-mm fixed on wings; 1 flexible in observer cockpit.
Ammunition:	
Bomb load:	160 light or 12 medium or 4 heavy.
Radio:	
Armor:	
Motors:	1 Piaggio P. XI RC. 40, 1,000 horsepower.
Maximum speed:	255 miles per hour.
Rate of climb:	1,380 feet per minute.
Service ceiling:	27,225 feet.
Range:	682 miles.
Wing span:	40 feet.

Fighter-Bomber
BREDA 65

ROYAL ITALIAN
AIR FORCE

SAVOIA-MARCHETTI SM 85

Description:	Round tip, slightly tapered, midwing mono-plane. All metal, twin motor, enclosed cock-pit, long blunt engine nacelles under the wings, retractable landing gear.
Crew:	1.
Armament:	1 Breda-Safat machine gun in floor of cockpit.
Ammunition:	
Bomb load:	Bombs carried under fuselage.
Radio:	
Armor:	
Motors:	2 1,000 horsepower Piaggio air-cooled.
Maximum speed:	317 miles per hour.
Rate of climb:	
Service ceiling:	
Range:	
Wing span:	

Dive Bomber-Ground Attack
SAVOIA-MARCHETTI SM 85

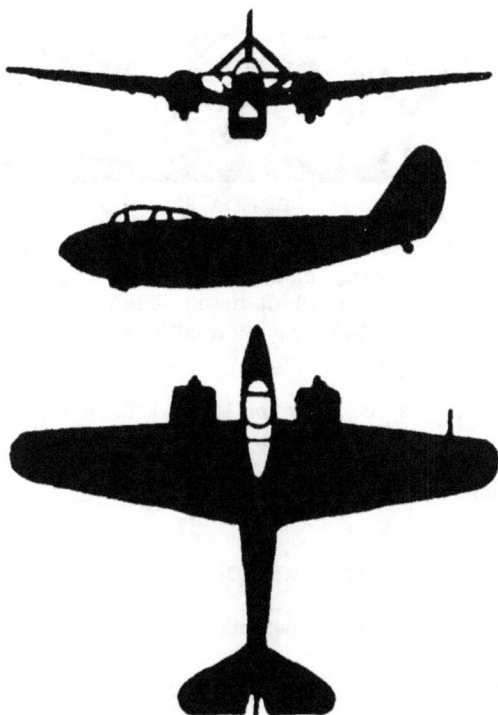

ROYAL ITALIAN
AIR FORCE

BREDA 88

Description:	Round tip, slightly swept-back, tapered, high-wing monoplane. All metal, twin motor, long blunt-nosed engine nacelles under wings, enclosed cockpit, retractable landing gear.
Crew:	2.
Armament:	2 fixed cannon, MA; 1 flexible gun in turret above wing.
Ammunition:	
Bomb load:	2,200 pounds.
Radio:	
Armor:	
Motors:	2 Piaggio XI. RC 40, 1,000 horsepower each.
Maximum speed:	352 miles per hour.
Rate of climb:	16,400 feet in 11 minutes.
Service ceiling:	26,000 feet.
Range:	1,120 miles.
Wing span:	51 feet.

Light Bomber
BREDA 88

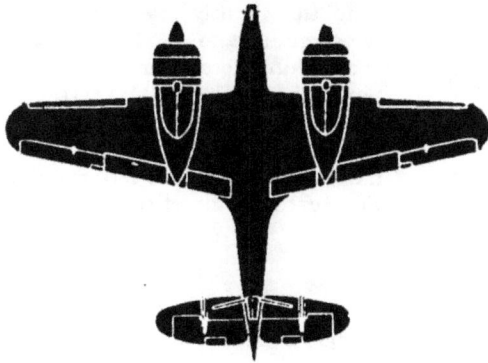

ROYAL ITALIAN
AIR FORCE

CAPRONI CA 311

Description: Round tip, slightly swept-back, tapered, low-
wing monoplane. Fabric covered, twin mo-
tor, blunt-nosed engine nacelles under
wings, enclosed cockpit, retractable landing
gear.
Crew: 3 or 4.
Armament: 1 fixed machine gun in left wing; 1 flexible in
gun turret on top of fuselage.
Ammunition:
Bomb load:
Radio: Two-way.
Armor:
Motors: 2 Piaggio P. XVI, 700 horsepower each.
Maximum
  speed: 270 miles per hour.
Rate of
  climb:
Service
  ceiling:
Range:
Wing span: 53⅙ feet.

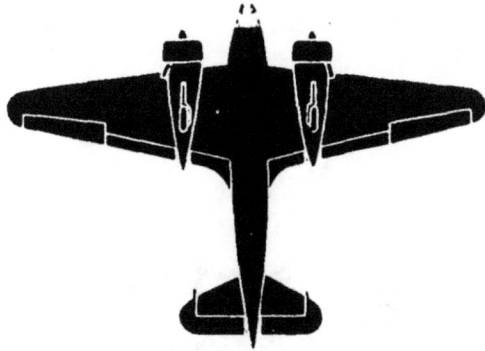

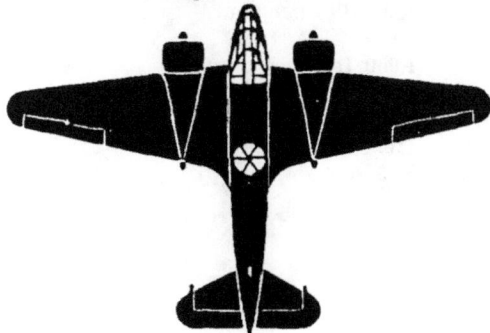

35

ROYAL ITALIAN
AIR FORCE

CANT Z 1007 BIS

Description: Round tip, tapered, dihedral, low-wing mono-
plane. Plywood fuselage, fabric wings, tri-
motor, long blunt nose, long blunt-nosed
engine nacelles under wings, enclosed cock-
pit, retractable landing gear.
Crew: 5.
Armament: 4 machine guns; 3 above, 1 below fuselage.
Ammunition:
Bomb load: 2,200 pounds.
Radio:
Armor:
Motors: 3 Piaggio P. XI RC. 40, 1,000 horsepower each.
Maximum
  speed: 280 miles per hour.
Rate of
  climb: 1,550 feet per minute.
Service
  ceiling: 26,200 feet.
Range: 1,372 miles.
Wing span: 81.3 feet.

Bomber
CANT Z 1007 BIS

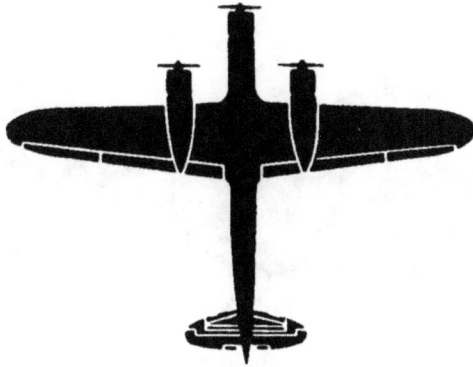

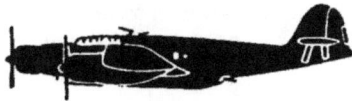

ROYAL ITALIAN
AIR FORCE

CANT Z 1011

Description:	Round tip; slightly dihedral, low-wing monoplane. Plywood construction, twin motor, long elliptical fuselage, engine nacelles above wing, enclosed, retractable landing gear. Twin rudders.
Crew:	5.
Armament:	4 machine guns in twin mountings, aft of wing, above and below fuselage.
Ammunition:	
Bomb load:	
Radio:	
Armor:	
Motors:	2 Isotta-Fraschini "Asso-XI R.C.," 840 horsepower each.
Maximum speed:	230 miles per hour.
Rate of climb:	16,400 feet in 19 minutes.
Service ceiling:	26,240 feet.
Range:	1,240 miles.
Wing span:	82 feet.

Bomber
CANT Z 1011

ROYAL ITALIAN
AIR FORCE

CAPRONI CA 135 BIS

Description: Round tip, slightly swept-back, tapered, midwing monoplane. Plywood wings, fabric
fuselage, twin motor, long elliptical fuselage,
long blunt-nosed engine nacelles set into
wings, enclosed, transparent section near tail,
retractable landing gear, twin fins and
rudders.

Crew: 5.

Armament: 1 machine gun in nose with lateral traverse;
1 machine gun in retractable turret on top
of fuselage; 1 machine gun under fuselage
behind wings.

Ammunition:

Bomb load: 1,760 pounds.

Radio:

Armor:

Motors: 2 Piaggio P. XI RC. 40, 1,000 horsepower each.

Maximum
  speed: 273 miles per hour.

Rate of
  climb: Initially 1,435 feet per minute.

Service
  ceiling: 22,960 feet.

Range: 1,240 miles.

Wing span: 61⅔ feet.

Bomber
CAPRONI CA 135 BIS

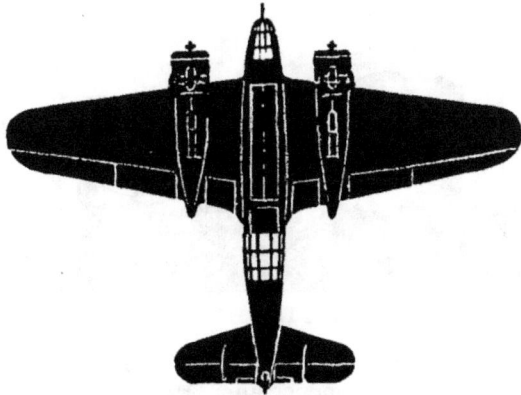

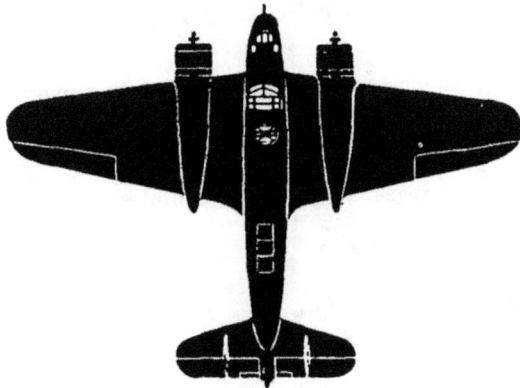

ROYAL ITALIAN
AIR FORCE

FIAT BR 20

Description: Round tip, slightly swept-back, tapered, low-
wing monoplane. Fabric, twin motor, long
elliptical fuselage, blunt-nosed engine nacelles built into wings, enclosed, retractable
landing gear, twin fins and rudders.

Crew: 4.

Armament: 1 machine gun in nose, 1 machine gun in retractable turret on top of fuselage; 1 machine gun at bottom at slight break in
bottom line of fuselage.

Ammunition:

Bomb load: 2,200 pounds.

Radio:

Armor:

Motors: 2 Fiat A 80 RC. 41, 1,000 horsepower each.

Maximum
  speed: 268 miles per hour.

Rate of
  climb: 19,680 feet in 22.5 minutes.

Service
  ceiling: 29,520 feet.

Maximum
  range: 1,863 miles.

Wing span: 70½ feet.

Bomber
FIAT BR 20

ROYAL ITALIAN
AIR FORCE

FIAT CR 25

Description:	Round tip, slightly swept-back, tapered, slightly negative dihedral low-wing monoplane. All metal, twin motor, long pointed nose, long blunt-nosed engine nacelles, set into wings, enclosed, retractable landing gear.
Crew:	3.
Armament:	2 fixed machine guns firing forward in nose; 1 machine gun in retractable turret on top of fuselage.
Ammunition:	
Bomb load:	
Radio:	
Armor:	
Motors:	2 Fiat A. 74 RC. 38, 840 horsepower each.
Maximum speed:	286 miles per hour.
Rate of climb:	19,680 feet in 12 minutes.
Service ceiling:	32,140 feet.
Range:	1,180 miles.
Wing span:	52 feet.

Bomber
FIAT CR 25

ROYAL ITALIAN
AIR FORCE

PIAGGIO P 32 MK II

Description:	Round tip, tapered, dihedral, midwing monoplane. Plywood structure, long elliptical nose, twin motor, blunt-nosed engine nacelles below wings, enclosed, retractable landing gear, twin fins and rudders.
Crew:	3.
Armament:	5 machine guns in turrets above and below fuselage.
Ammunition:	
Bomb load:	3,520 pounds.
Radio:	
Armor:	
Motors:	2 Piaggio P. XI RC. 40, 1,020 horsepower each.
Maximum speed:	264 miles per hour.
Rate of climb:	13,120 feet in 15 minutes.
Service ceiling:	26,240 feet.
Range:	1,875 miles.
Wing span:	59 feet.

Bomber
PIAGGIO P 32 MK II

ROYAL ITALIAN
AIR FORCE

SAVOIA MARCHETTI SM 79

Description:	Round tip, slightly swept-back, tapered, straight, low-wing monoplane. Front part of fuselage only metaled, rest plywood and fabric construction, enclosed, trimotor, long blunt-nosed fuselage, engine nacelles below wings, retractable landing gear.
Crew:	4.
Armament:	1 machine gun firing forward; 2 machine guns on movable mounts, 1 above and 1 below fuselage behind wings; 1 machine gun on sliding mount inside rear portion fuselage.
Ammunition:	
Bomb load:	2,200 pounds.
Radio:	
Armor:	
Motors:	3 Piaggio P. XI RC. 40, 1,000 horsepower each.
Maximum speed:	295 miles per hour.
Rate of climb:	16,400 feet in 19.75 minutes.
Service ceiling:	27,880 feet.
Range:	1,240 miles.
Wing span:	66¼ feet.

Bomber-Reconnaissance
SAVOIA MARCHETTI SM 79

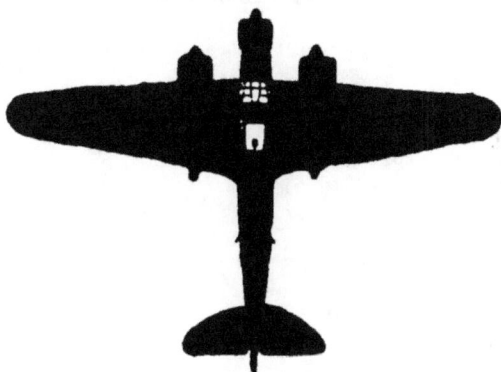

ROYAL ITALIAN
AIR FORCE

SAVOIA MARCHETTI SM 81

Description: Round tip swept-back, dihedral, low-wing
monoplane. Trimotor, long blunt nose, en-
gine nacelles set into wing, enclosed, fixed
landing gear.
Crew:
Armament: 4 7.7-mm machine guns on flexible mounts.
Ammunition:
Bomb load: 2,200 pounds.
Radio:
Armor:
Motors: 3 Piaggio P. XI RC. 40, 1,000 horsepower each.
Maximum 202 miles per hour.
  speed:
Rate of
  climb:
Service 24,600 feet.
  ceiling:
Range: 1,240 miles.
Wing span: $78\frac{2}{3}$ feet.

Bomber-Reconnaissance
SAVOIA MARCHETTI SM 81

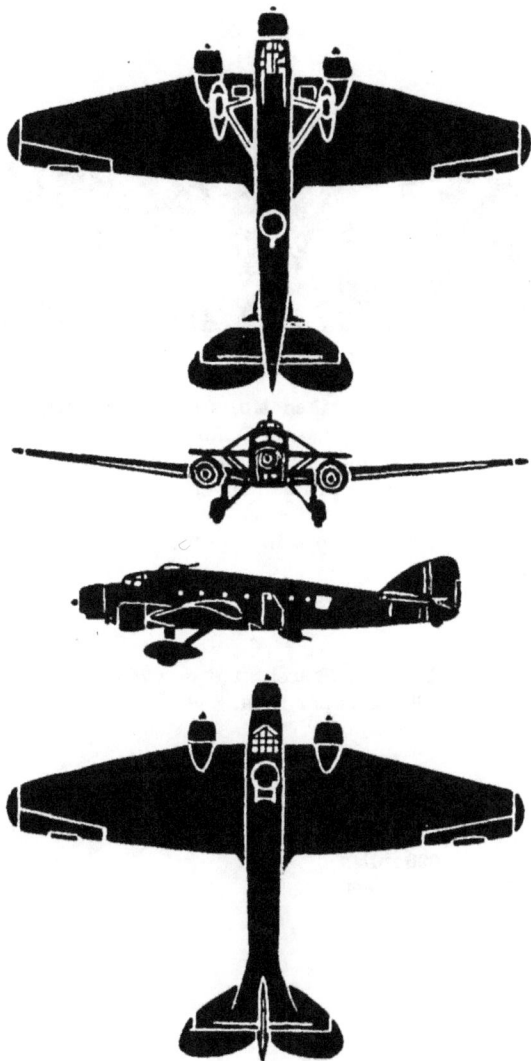

ROYAL ITALIAN
AIR FORCE

CAPRONI CA 111

Description: Slightly raked tip, straight, slightly dihedral,
high-wing monoplane. Fabric covering, sin-
gle motor, rounded nose, fixed undercar-
riage; can be converted to seaplane.

Crew:

Armament: 4 7.7-mm machine guns.

Ammunition:

Bomb load: 1,100 pounds.

Radio:

Armor:

Motors: 1 Isotta-Fraschini Asso, 750 horsepower.

Maximum
speed: 180 miles per hour.

Rate of
climb: 9,800 feet in 14.5 minutes.

Service
ceiling: 21,300 feet.

Range: 620 miles.

Wing span: 75½ feet.

Reconnaissance
CAPRONI CA 111

ROYAL ITALIAN
AIR FORCE

CAPRONI CA 310 LIBECCIO

Description:	Round tip, slightly swept-back, tapered, slightly dihedral, low-wing monoplane. Wooden wings, fabric fuselage, twin motor, long pointed nose, transparent panels underneath, engine nacelles set into wings, retractable landing gear.
Crew:	3.
Armament:	2 fixed machine guns in wing roots; 1 flexible in retractable turret on top of fuselage.
Ammunition:	
Bomb load:	880 pounds.
Radio:	
Armor:	
Motors:	2 Piaggio P. VII C. 35, 470 horsepower each.
Maximum speed:	230 miles per hour.
Rate of climb:	Initially 1,000 feet per minute.
Service ceiling:	23,000 feet.
Range:	750 miles.
Wing span:	$53\frac{1}{6}$ feet.

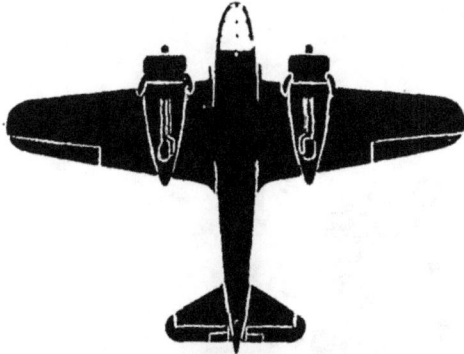

ROYAL ITALIAN
AIR FORCE

CAPRONI CA 134

Description: Round tip, staggered, straight-wing biplane.
Single motor, long pointed nose, twin fins
and rudders, fixed landing gear.

Crew: 2.
Armament:
Ammunition:
Bomb load:
Radio:
Armor:
Motors: 1 Isotta-Fraschini, 900 horsepower.
Maximum
 speed: 242 miles per hour.
Rate of
 climb:
Service
 ceiling: 26,240 feet.
Range:
Wing span: 31¼ feet.

Army Cooperation
CAPRONI CA 134

ROYAL ITALIAN
AIR FORCE ·

CAPRONI CA 164

Description: Round tip, straight-wing, slightly dihedral,
biplane of unequal span. Single motor,
long pointed nose, fixed landing gear, open
cockpit.

Crew: 1.
Armament:
Ammunition:
Bomb load:
Radio:
Armor:
Motors: 1.
Maximum
  speed:
Rate of
  climb:
Service
  ceiling:
Range:
Wing span:

Army Cooperation
CAPRONI CA 164

ROYAL ITALIAN
AIR FORCE

MERIDIONALI RO 37 BIS

Description: Round tip, straight-wing, cut-out, staggered biplane of unequal span. Fuselage partially metaled, remaining structure fabric, single motor, blunt nose, enclosed cockpit, fixed landing gear.

Crew: 2.

Armament: 2 Breda-Safat machine guns fixed firing through propeller; 1 Breda-Safat on flexible mount over rear cockpit.

Ammunition:

Bomb load: 12 33-pound bombs.

Radio:

Armor:

Motors: 1 Piaggio P. XR, 700 horsepower, or 1 Piaggio P. IXr. C., 560 horsepower.

Maximum
  speed: 205 miles per hour.

Rate of
  climb: 19,680 feet in 16 minutes.

Service
  ceiling: 24,930 feet.

Range: 1,090 miles.

Wing span: 36⅓ feet.

Army Cooperation
MERIDIONALI RO 37 BIS

ROYAL ITALIAN
AIR FORCE

CAPRONI CA 133

Description: Raked tip, straight-wing, slightly dihedral, braced high-wing monoplane. Front part of fuselage metaled, remaining structure fabric, trimotor, long tapered nose, engine nacelles below wings, enclosed; fixed landing gear.

Crew: 2; 16 passengers.
Armament: 4 flexible 7.7-mm machine guns.
Ammunition:
Bomb load:
Radio:
Armor:
Motors: 3 Piaggio "Stella" VI RC., 370 horsepower each.
Maximum
  speed: 174 miles per hour.
Rate of
  climb: 16,400 feet in 21 minutes.
Service
  ceiling: 21,320 feet.
Range: 838 miles.
Wing span: 69⅔ feet.

Transport
CAPRONI CA 133

ROYAL ITALIAN
AIR FORCE

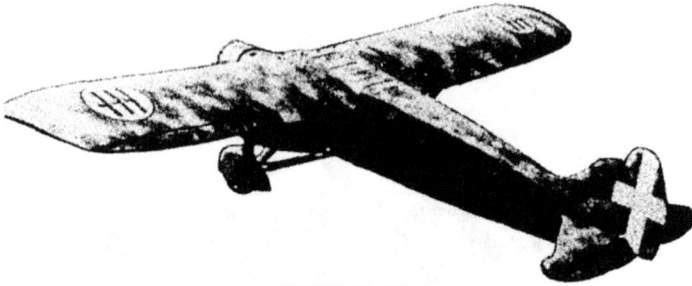

FIAT G 18

Description:	Round tip, slightly swept-back, tapered, dihedral low-wing monoplane. Long pointed nose, twin motor, engine nacelles set into wings, enclosed, fixed landing gear.
Crew:	3; 18 passengers.
Armament:	
Ammunition:	
Bomb load:	
Radio:	
Armor:	
Motors:	2 Fiat, 1,000 horsepower each.
Maximum speed:	250 miles per hour.
Rate of climb:	
Service ceiling:	28,680 feet.
Range:	930 miles.
Wing span:	82 feet.

Transport
FIAT G 18

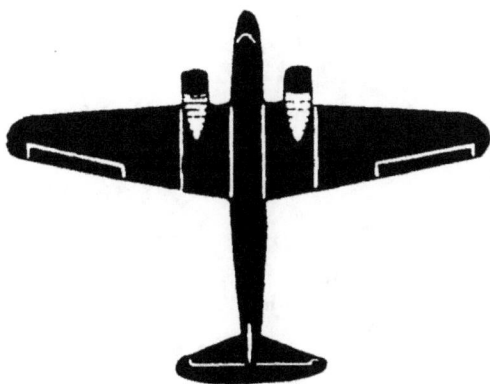

ROYAL ITALIAN
AIR FORCE

SAVOIA MARCHETTI SM 73

Description: Round tip, swept-back, slightly tapered, low-wing monoplane. Long blunt nose, engine nacelles set into wings, fixed landing gear, trimotor.

Crew: 4; 18 passengers.
Armament:
Ammunition:
Bomb load:
Radio:
Armor:
Motors: 3 Alfa-Romeo, 750 horsepower each.
Maximum
   speed: 200 miles per hour.
Rate of
   climb:
Service
   ceiling: 20,000 feet.
Range: 625–1,250 miles.
Wing span: 79 feet.

66

Transport
SAVOIA MARCHETTI SM 73

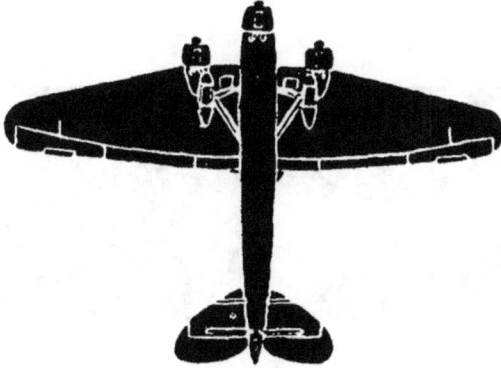

ROYAL ITALIAN
AIR FORCE

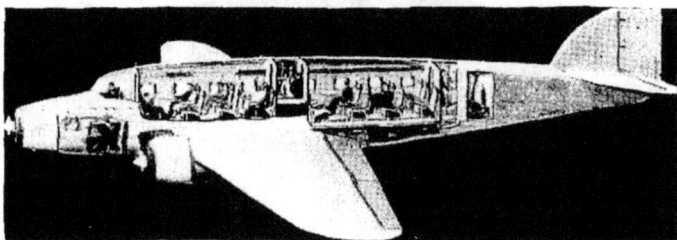

SAVOIA MARCHETTI SM 75

Description: Round tip, swept-back, tapered, low-wing
monoplane. Front part of fuselage met-
aled, remaining structure plywood and
fabric, trimotor, long tapered nose, enclosed,
retractable landing gear.

Crew: 3; 24 passengers.
Armament:
Ammunition:
Bomb load:
Radio:
Armor:
Motors: 3 Alfa-Romeo, 750 horsepower each.
Maximum
  speed: 230 miles per hour.
Rate of climb:
Service
  ceiling: 25,570 feet.
Maximum
  range: 875 miles.
Wing span: 97½ feet.

Transport
SAVOIA MARCHETTI SM 75

ROYAL ITALIAN
AIR FORCE

SAVOIA MARCHETTI SM 82
"MARSUPIALE"

Description: Round tip, swept-back, tapered, slightly dihedral, midwing monoplane. Trimotor, long
blunt nose, engine nacelles below wing, enclosed, retractable landing gear.

Crew:
Armament:
Ammunition:
Bomb load:
Radio:
Armor:
Motors: 3, 950 horsepower each.
Maximum
   speed: 230 miles per hour.
Rate of
   climb:
Service
   ceiling:
Range: 2,480 miles (has flown 8,040 miles in 57 hours).
Wing span: 97½ feet.

Transport
SAVOIA MARCHETTI SM 82 "MARSUPIALE"

ROYAL ITALIAN
AIR FORCE

SAVOIA MARCHETTI SM 83

Description: Round tip, slightly swept-back, tapered, low-
              wing monoplane. Front part of fuselage
              metaled, remaining structure wood and
              fabric, trimotor, long blunt nose, engine na-
              celles below wings, enclosed, retractable
              landing gear.
Crew: 4; 10 passengers.
Armament:
Ammunition:
Bomb load:
Radio:
Armor:
Motors: 3 Alfa-Romeo 126 RC. 34, 750 horsepower each.
Maximum
  speed: 276 miles per hour.
Rate of
  climb: 13,120 feet in 13.5 minutes.
Service
  ceiling: 27,600 feet.
Range: 930 miles.
Wing span: 69¾ feet.

Transport
SAVOIA MARCHETTI SM 83

ROYAL ITALIAN
AIR FORCE

CAPRONI GHIBLI

Description: Round tip, tapered, slightly negative dihedral, low-wing monoplane. Long pointed nose, twin motor, engine nacelles below wings, enclosed, fixed landing gear.

Crew: 3.
Armament:
Ammunition:
Bomb load: 750 pounds.
Radio:
Armor:
Motors: 2 Alfa-Romeo, 200 horsepower each.
Maximum
  speed: 160 miles per hour.
Rate of
  climb:
Service
  ceiling: 14,760 feet.
Range: 962 miles.
Wing span: 53¼ feet.

General Purpose
CAPRONI GHIBLI

ROYAL ITALIAN
AIR FORCE

NARDI F. N. 315

Description: Round tip, distinctly swept-back and tapered,
               low-wing monoplane. Long blunt nose, sin-
               gle motor, enclosed, retractable landing gear.
Crew: 2.
Armament: 2 machine guns.
Ammunition:
Bomb load:
Radio:
Armor:
Motors: 1 Hirth, 260 horsepower.
Maximum
  speed: 240 miles per hour.
Rate of
  climb:
Service
  ceiling:
Range: 600 miles.
Wing span: 27¾ feet.

General Purpose
NARDI F. N. 315

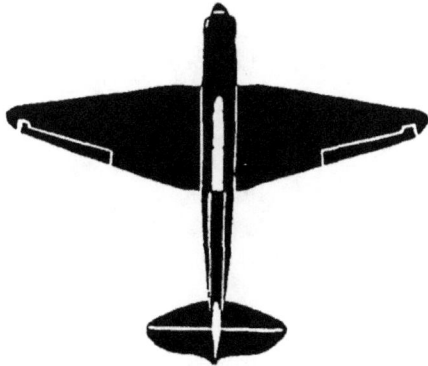

IDENTIFICATION OF ITALIAN AIRCRAFT

SEAPLANES

ROYAL ITALIAN
AIR FORCE

MERIDIONALI RO 44

Description: Round tip, gull wing, staggered biplane of un-
              equal span with single float for catapult
              launching. Fuselage partially metaled, re-
              maining construction fabric, blunt-nosed,
              enclosed.

Crew: 1.

Armament: 2 12.7-mm Breda-Safat machine guns fixed
              firing through propeller.

Ammunition:

Bomb load:

Radio:

Armor:

Motors: 1 Piaggio P. X. R., 700 horsepower.

Maximum
  speed: 190 miles per hour.

Rate of
  climb: 16,400 feet in 12.5 minutes.

Service
  ceiling: 23,000 feet.

Range: 300 miles.

Wing span: 38 feet.

Fighter Seaplane
MERIDIONALI RO 44

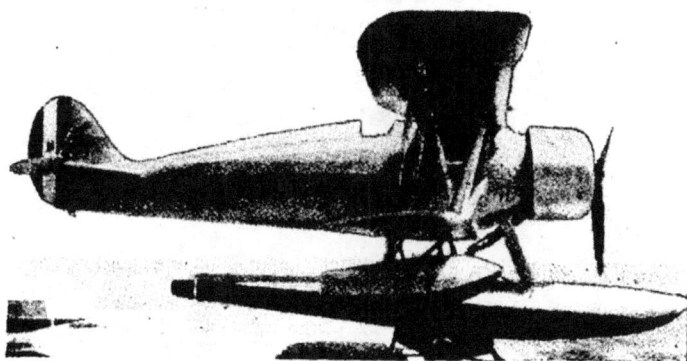

ROYAL ITALIAN
AIR FORCE

MERIDIONALI RO 43

Description: Elliptical tip, straight wing, cut-out, gull-wing biplane of unequal span fitted with single float fixed for catapult launching. Fuselage partially metaled, remaining structure fabric, single motor, blunt nose, enclosed cockpit.

Crew: 2.

Armament: 2 fixed Breda-Safat machine guns firing through propeller; 1 Breda-Safat flexible over rear cockpit.

Ammunition:

Bomb load:

Radio:

Armor:

Motors: 1 Piaggio P. X. R., 700 horsepower.

Maximum
   speed: 196 miles per hour.

Rate of
   climb: 16,400 feet in 12.8 minutes.

Service
   ceiling: 21,650 feet.

Range: 930 miles.

Wing span: 38 feet.

Fighter Reconnaissance Seaplane
MERIDIONALI RO 43

ROYAL ITALIAN
AIR FORCE

CANT Z 501

Description: Elliptical, straight, high-wing monoplane flying boat. Semicircular two step hull of
wood, fabric wings, enclosed, single motor,
engine nacelle above hull set into and above
wing.

Crew: 4.
Armament: 1 machine gun in nose cockpit; 2 in engine
                nacelle position; 1 in rear cockpit.
Ammunition:
Bomb load: 1,100 pounds.
Radio:
Armor:
Motors: 1 Isotta-Fraschini Asso-XI RC. 15, 840 horse-
                power.
Maximum
  speed: 170 miles per hour.
Rate of
  climb: 13,120 feet in 16 minutes.
Service
  ceiling:
Range: 620 miles.
Wing span: 74 feet.

Reconnaissance-Bomber Flying Boat
CANT Z 501

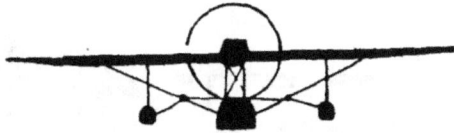

ROYAL ITALIAN
AIR FORCE

CANT Z 506B

Description:	Elliptical tip, tapered, dihedral midwing monoplane fitted with twin single-step metal floats. W o o d e n construction, trimotor, short blunt nose, long bulge under fuselage, engine nacelles set into wing.
Crew:	6.
Armament:	4 Breda-Safat 12.7-mm machine guns.
Ammunition:	350 rounds per gun.
Bomb load:	
Radio:	
Armor:	
Motors:	3 Alfa-Romeo 126 RC. 34, 750 horsepower each.
Maximum speed:	236 miles per hour.
Rate of climb:	Initially 820 feet per minute.
Service ceiling:	24,500 feet.
Range:	1,240 miles.
Wing span:	87 feet.

Reconnaissance-Bomber Seaplane
CANT Z 506B

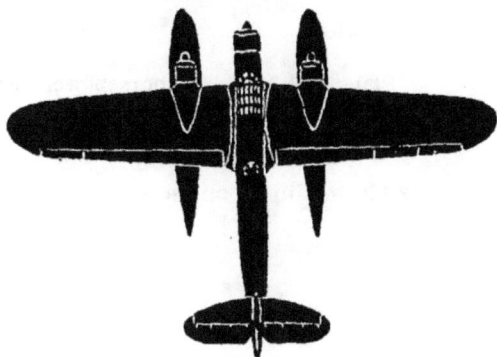

ROYAL ITALIAN
AIR FORCE

CAPRONI CA 312 BIS

Description: Round tip, tapered, dihedral, low-wing mono-
      plane fitted with two long single-step metal
      floats. Fabric fuselage, wood wings, twin
      motor, rounded fuselage with transparent
      nose, enclosed, engine nacelles set into
      wings. May be used to drop torpedoes.

Crew: 3.

Armament: 1 fixed 7.7-mm machine gun mounted on left
      wing; 1 flexible 7.7-mm machine gun in
      revolving turret on top of fuselage.

Ammunition:

Bomb load:

Radio: Two-way.

Armor:

Motors: 2 Piaggio P XVI, 630 horsepower each.

Maximum
 speed: 248 miles per hour.

Rate of
 climb: 13,120 feet in 13 minutes.

Service
 ceiling: 19,680 feet.

Range: 560 miles.

Wing span: 54 feet.

Reconnaissance-Bomber Seaplane
CAPRONI CA 312 BIS

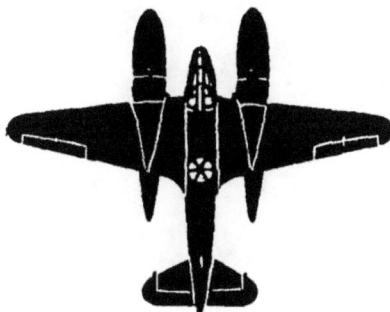

ROYAL ITALIAN
AIR FORCE

FIAT R. S. 14

Description: Round tip, tapered, dihedral, midwing monoplane fitted with twin metal floats. All
metal, twin motor, long pointed nose with
transparent section, enclosed, engine nacelles
set into wings.

Crew:
Armament:
Ammunition:
Bomb load:
Radio:
Armor:
Motors: 2.
Maximum
  speed:
Rate of
  climb:
Service
  ceiling:
Range:
Wing span:

IDENTIFICATION OF ITALIAN AIRCRAFT

Reconnaissance-Bomber Seaplane
FIAT R. S. 14

www.ingramcontent.com/pod-product-compliance
Lightning Source LLC
LaVergne TN
LVHW051704080426
835511LV00017B/2717